Did It?

by Wiley Blevins
illustrated by Chris Chatterton

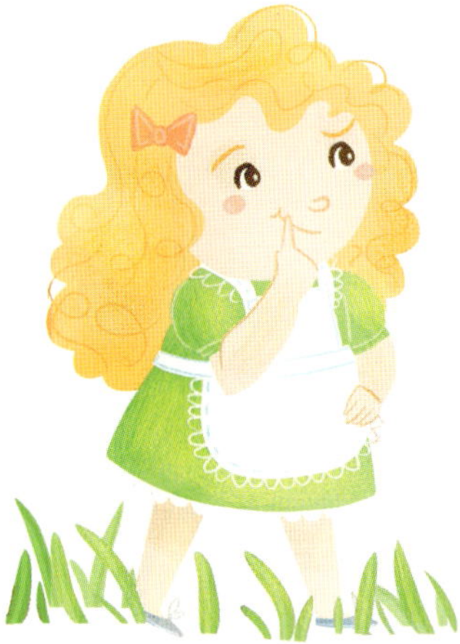

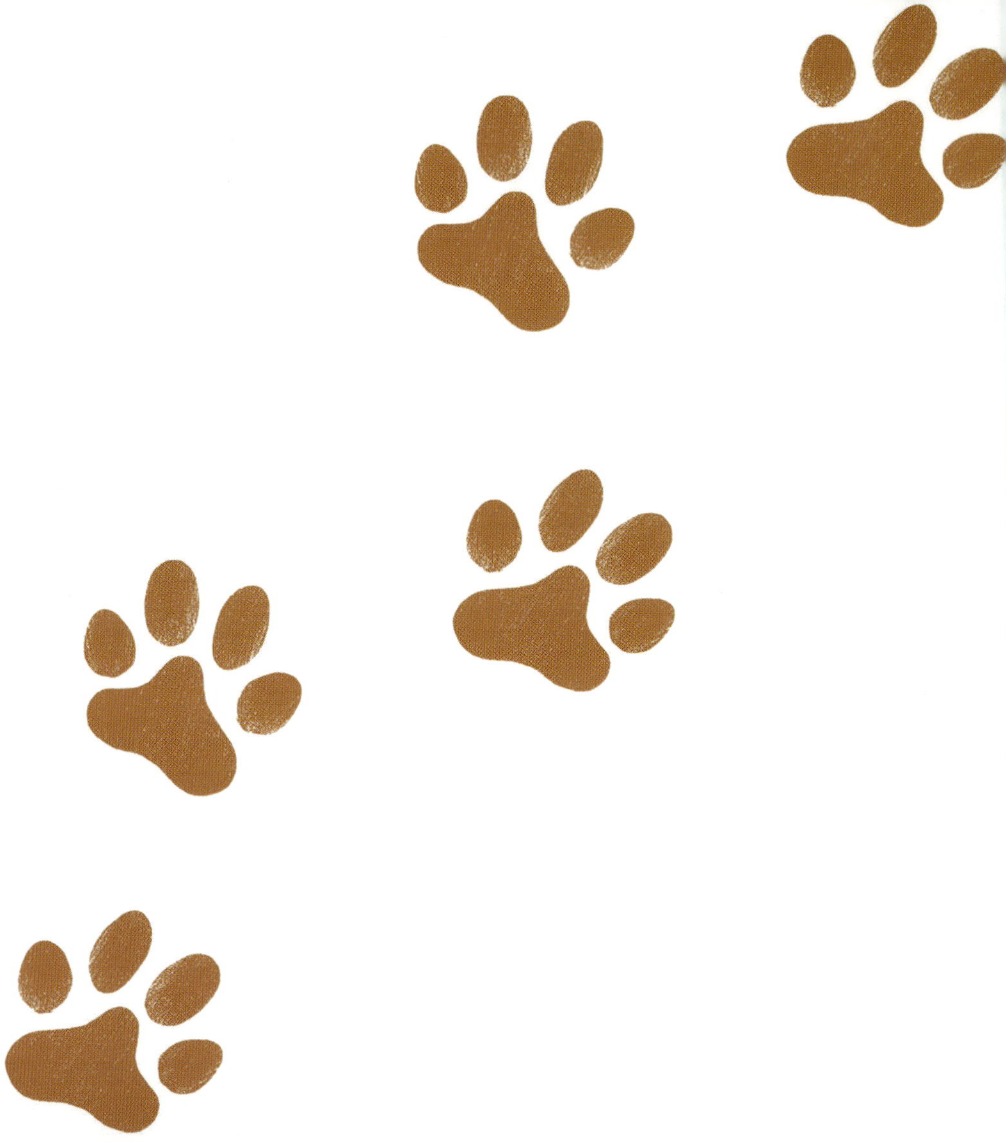

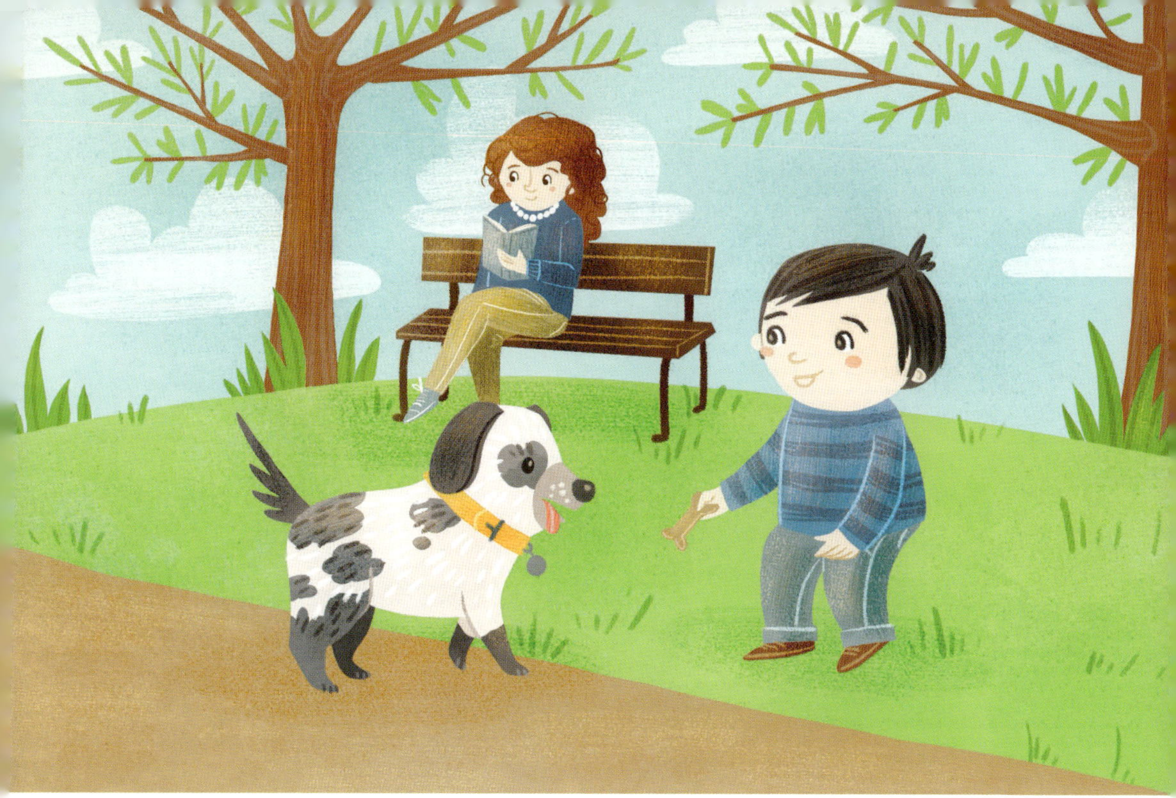

Did the dog sit?

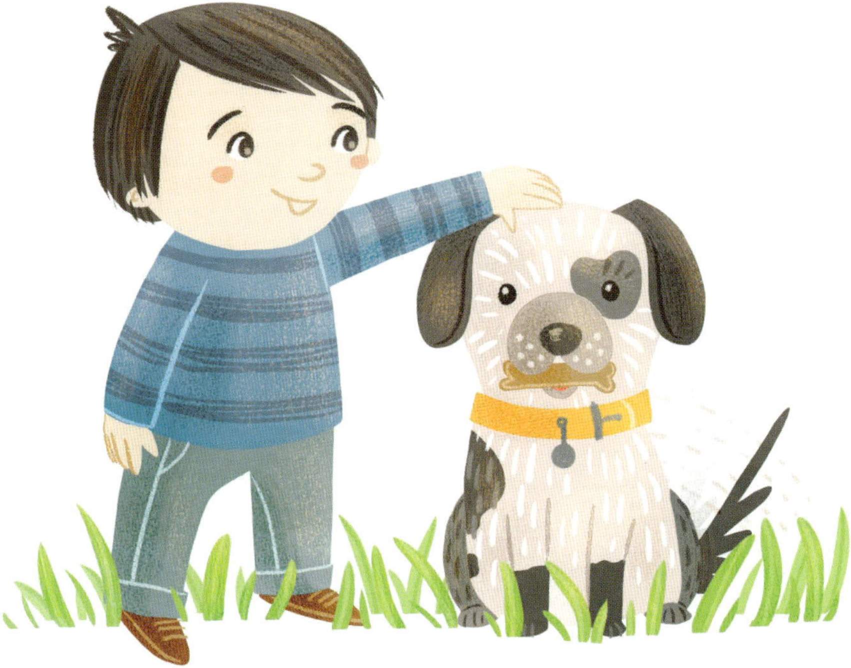

It did!

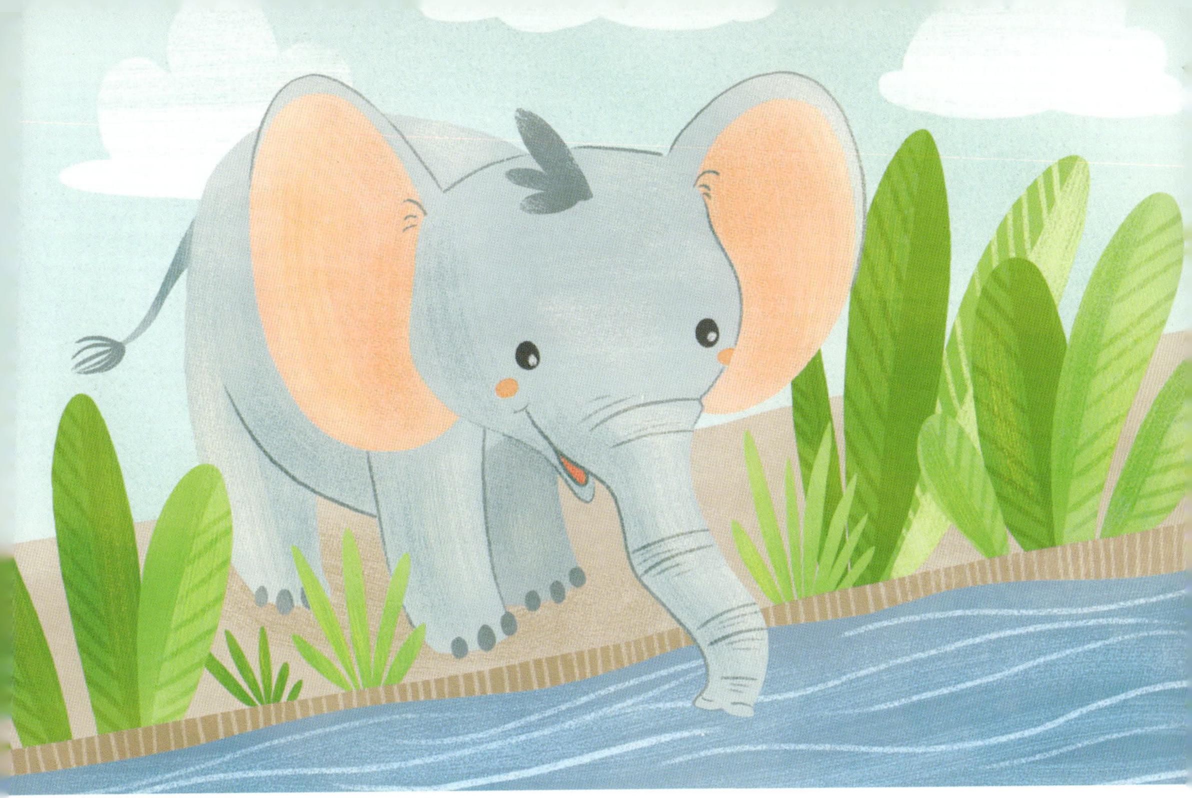

Did the elephant sit?

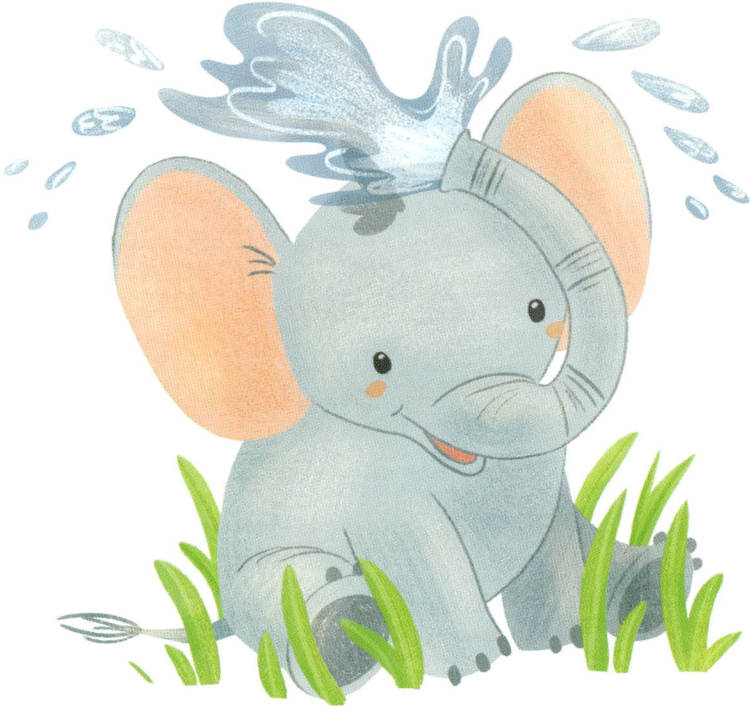

It did.

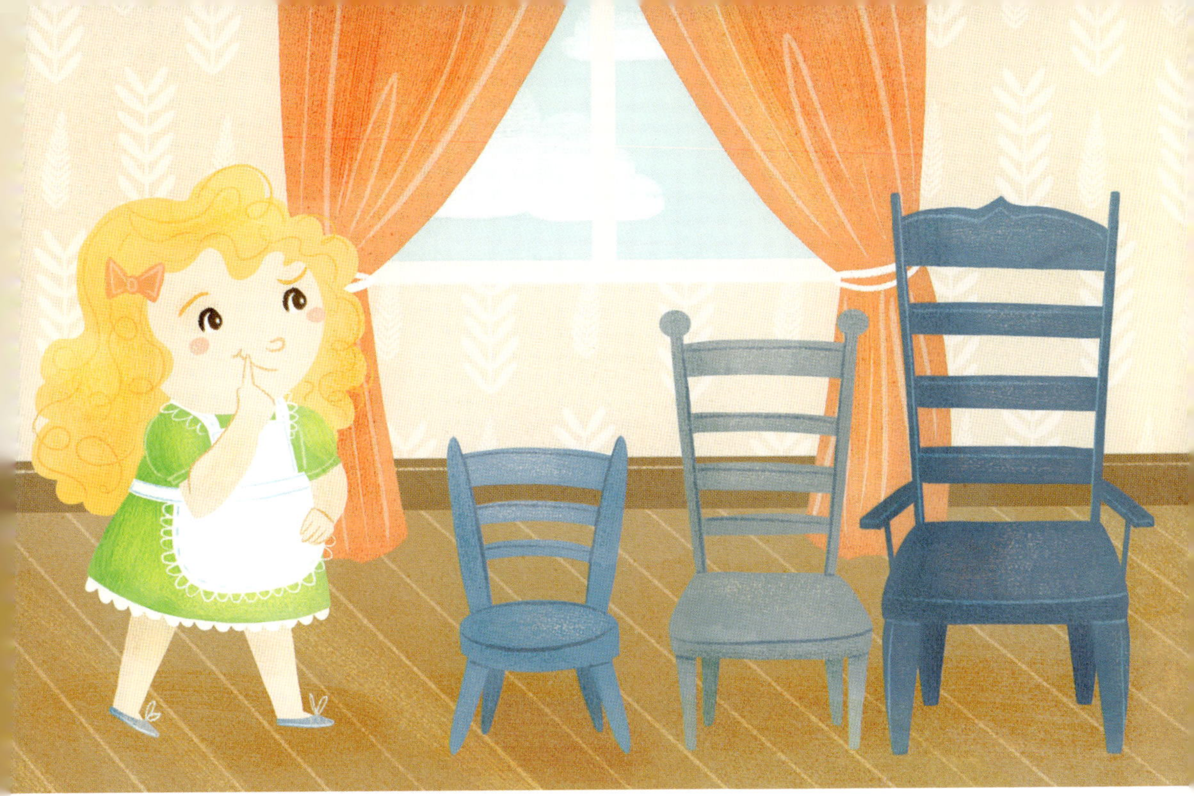

Did Goldilocks sit?

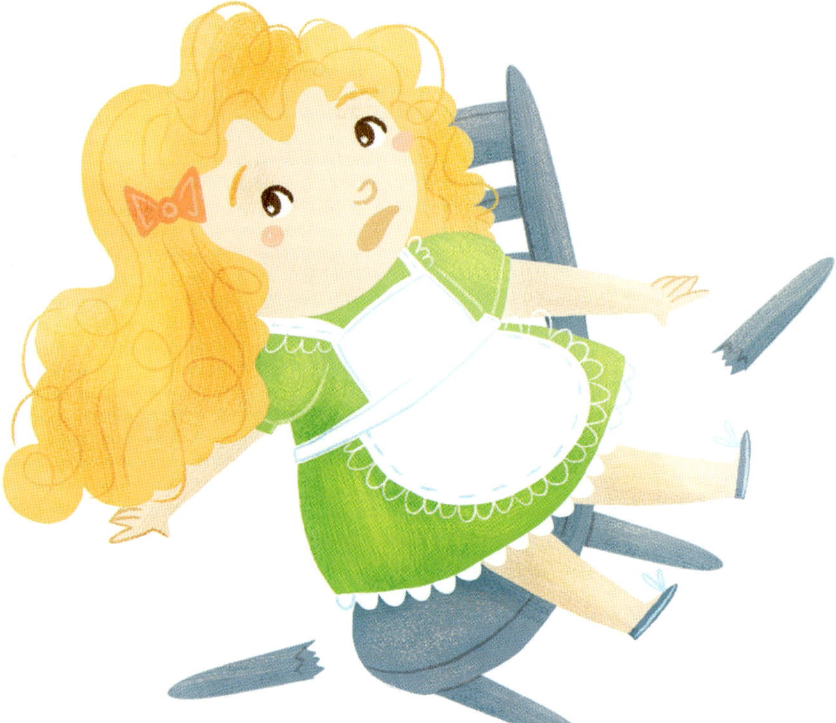

She did!